A BUSINESS AND ITS BELIEFS

A Business and Its Beliefs

The Ideas That Helped Build IBM

Thomas J. Watson, Jr.
Former Chairman of the Board
International Business Machines Corporations

McGraw-Hill
New York Chicago San Francisco
Lisbon London Madrid Mexico City Milan
New Delhi San Juan Seoul Singapore
Sydney Toronto

CONTENTS

"I firmly believe that any organization, in order to achieve success, must have a sound set of beliefs on which it premises all its policies and actions."

"The relationship between the man and the customer, their mutual trust, the importance of reputation, the idea of putting the customer first—always—all these things, if carried out with real conviction by a company, can make a great deal of difference in its destiny."

"To keep a company ethical and clean is the responsibility of top management. It can never be left to chance."

PUBLISHER'S NOTE

A *Business and Its Beliefs* was first published by McGraw-Hill in 1963 and quickly became an important part of the management literature of the day. It is considered one of those rare books that is as relevant today as it was when it was first published four decades earlier. Not only were Thomas Watson, Jr. and his father prescient, but they also gave voice to many ideas and principles that other companies and CEOs would adapt many years later. It is for this reason that McGraw-Hill has decided to reissue this classic leadership volume.

When Mr. Watson, the son of the legendary founder Thomas J. Watson, Sr., wrote the book, he was chairman of the board of IBM, having also served as the company's president and CEO. The premise of this important work is clear and straightforward: that all great institutions require a set of principles and beliefs to guide them through good times and bad. And the most important determinant of a company's success depends on its "faithful adherence" to these bedrock beliefs.

At IBM, Mr. Watson felt that three core beliefs formed the foundation for the company's success:

- Have respect for the individual.
- Give the best company service of any company in the world.
- Pursue all tasks with the idea that they can be accomplished in a superior fashion.

Have Respect for the Individual

Thomas Watson, Jr. said that respect for the individual

"was deep bone in my father." Both father and son believed that an organization owed a special responsibility to its people, and both spent a majority of their time making sure that employees were treated with dignity. This belief was born out of Thomas Watson, Sr.'s own experience. Early on in his career he was fired from a company called National Cash, but later he was called in to run a company called Computing-Tabulating-Recording Company, a series of three small companies that would become IBM a decade later.

Respect for the individual took many forms at IBM. It meant having an "open door" policy, long before other firms would adopt such a measure. Thomas Watson, Jr. "recognized that the individual has his own problems, ambitions, abilities, frustrations, and goals." As a result, managers were expected to work with employees, assist them on sales calls, and know how to train them. Also, Watson felt strongly that there should be "continual opportunity for advancement" and key management positions should be filled from within the company.

Lastly, Watson felt that IBM needed its share of "wild ducks." To better understand the origins of this philosophy, one will have to read the book. Suffice to say that Watson knew that complacency was the enemy of the organization, and he worked to make sure that the company had its share of wild ducks.

Give the Best Company Service of Any Company in the World

In its early years, IBM ran an advertisement that Watson felt summed up another key company philosophy: "IBM Means Service." To the IBM founders, this meant giving the "best service of any company in the world." One of the origins of this lofty and important goal was the early career of Thomas Watson, Sr. When he was 18, he sold pianos and sewing machines in the countryside. Farmers, almost always short of cash, traded farm equipment or livestock for Watson's goods. This embedded in him a keen understanding of how to please customers, even those incapable of "paying" for his products.

At IBM, granting excellent customer service was the responsibility of IBM's sales and service forces, but "that good service . . . requires the cooperation of all parts of the business." Thomas Watson, Jr. stated unequivocally "a reputation for service is one of the company's principal assets." He also said that ultimately service became a "reflex" at IBM.

Pursue All Tasks with the Idea That They Can Be Accomplished in a Superior Fashion

"IBM expects and demands superior performance from its people in whatever it does," proclaimed Thomas Watson, Jr. He added that this sort of environment is never easy, but aiming for perfection will put organizations on the proper path. Watson also added that it is incumbent upon corporations to aim for seemingly impossible tasks. We see, once again, that Watson was ahead of his time. Decades later, other CEOs attracted attention for establishing "stretch goals," something that IBM had been issuing since the first half of the 20th century.

Thomas Watson, Sr. used to tell his employees "It is better to aim at perfection and miss than it is to aim at perfection and hit it." This set a tone of "optimism, enthusiasm, excitement and pace." The company constantly strived to do things better, to find a way to improve on everything it did, from new products to slogans to sales contests. It was this optimistic tone that led the senior Watson to hire salesmen even during the Depression. He told a competitor that men of his age always do something "foolish." He added "some men play too much poker, and others bet on horse races . . . my hobby is hiring salespeople." When business conditions improved the following year and boomed after the war, Thomas Watson appeared to be not so foolish after all.

It is now a commonly accepted truism that the corporation is more than a legal entity engaged in the production and sale of goods and services for profit. It is also the embodiment of the principles and beliefs of the men and women who give it substance. More particularly, the corporation is the expression of those who have given it leadership in its development and in the conduct of its affairs.

Perhaps no corporation is more illustrative of these characteristics than the International Business Machines Corporation. Engaged as it is in advanced scientific development, as an organization it is nevertheless governed in its daily affairs by the verities of human relations. Enduring truths of personal conduct learned early by the company's founder in an uncomplicated rural community setting have successfully served as management guidelines in the development of a highly complex business organization which operates in the most scientific areas of contemporary times.

The interesting story of this remarkable experience in the business world is told with perception and enthusiasm by the Corporation's present chief executive officer, Mr. Thomas J. Watson, Jr. Technological change in its field has been unbelievably rapid, and the growth of the company has been remarkable. In fifteen postwar years gross sales have increased by a factor of fourteen. It is one thing to hold firmly to guiding beliefs in a static situation; it is harder to do so in a dynamic and ever-changing one. Respect for the individual may be just as great, but it is far more difficult to assure that it is given expression. Dedication to service acquires new dimensions and takes new forms, and the task of convincing new employees of its prime importance is formidable. The effort to achieve superiority in all activities is progressively more challenged as the range of activity is extended. The manner in which management has adapted its basic beliefs to the company's rapid development serves convincingly to reaffirm their validity.

These essays have grown out of the lectures presented at the Columbia Graduate School of Business in the spring of 1962. Sponsored jointly by the School and the McKinsey Foundation for Management Research, Inc., they were part of the continuing series on the management of large organizations that has become so well known in recent years.

The thinking of a man with the inquisitive and vigorous mind of Mr. Watson would naturally extend beyond the boundaries of internal company affairs. His observations on the role of the modern corporation in the society that gives it sanction share equal place with his insights on business management. The reader of this volume will find it to be a forthright expression of the enlightened attitudes of business leaders in the Western World—attitudes that serve as our most effective defense of the free way of life.

Courtney C. Brown
Dean, Graduate School of Business
Columbia University

A BUSINESS AND ITS BELIEFS

Part I

**THE HERITAGE
AND THE CHALLENGE**

1

BRINGING OUT THE BEST

Of the top twenty-five industrial corporations in the United States in 1900, only two remain in that select company today. One retains its original identity; the other is a merger of seven corporations on that original list. Two of those twenty-five failed. Three others merged and dropped behind. The remaining twelve have continued in business, but each has fallen substantially in its standing.

Figures like these help to remind us that corporations are expendable and that success—at best—is an impermanent achievement which can always slip out of hand.

One may speculate at length as to the cause of the decline or fall of a corporation. Technology, changing tastes, changing fashions, all play a part. But the fact remains that some companies manage to flourish while others in the very same industry may falter or fail. Normally we ascribe these differences to such things as business competence, market judgment, and the quality of leadership in a corporation. Each one of these is a vital factor. No one can dispute their importance. But I question whether they in themselves are decisive.

I believe the real difference between success and failure in a corporation can very often be traced to the question of how well the organization brings out the great energies and talents of its people. What does it do to help these people find common cause with each other? How does it keep them pointed in the right direction despite the many rivalries and differences which may exist among them? And how can it sustain this common cause and sense of direction through the many changes which take place from one generation to another?

These problems are not unique to corporations. They exist in all large organizations, in political and

4

religious institutions. Consider any great organization—one that has lasted over the years—and I think you will find that it owes its resiliency, not to its form of organization or administrative skills, but to the power of what we call *beliefs* and the appeal these beliefs have for its people.

This, then, is my thesis: I firmly believe that any organization, in order to survive and achieve success, must have a sound set of beliefs on which it premises all its policies and actions.

Next, I believe that the most important single factor in corporate success is faithful adherence to those beliefs.

And finally, I believe that if an organization is to meet the challenges of a changing world, it must be prepared to change everything about itself except those beliefs as it moves through corporate life.

In other words, the basic philosophy, spirit, and drive of an organization have far more to do with its relative achievements than do technological or economic resources, organizational structure, innovation, and timing. All these things weigh heavily in success. But they are, I think, transcended by how strongly the people in the organization believe in its basic precepts and how faithfully they carry them out.

IBM, I think, offers some evidence of how an organization's beliefs can help it to grow and prosper. Not one of the beliefs I shall talk about is unique, though IBM's approach to them may be unusual. At any rate, I offer them for whatever value they may have for other organizations. Initially I shall examine these beliefs to see how they have been developed and applied. Thereafter I shall expand the thesis with some views on the broader responsibilities of American business.

Some may say that our experience has been unique, that IBM has been successful only because it has had an unusual market and because it has been in that market long enough to establish deeper roots than some other organizations. As a consequence, this argument goes, even befuddled management could have moved a company to the point that we have moved our. Obviously we don't believe this.

It is true that we have enjoyed more than the usual measure of success. Of course being in the right place at the right time with the right product has helped a lot; yet I do not think this has been the decisive factor. I attribute our success in the main to the power of IBM's beliefs. This is not to say for a moment that our philosophy is the only one for business. Although I hope that it may prove useful to others, I have no gospel to spread outside IBM.

During the early period of IBM's development—from 1914 to 1945—while its beliefs were being formed, tested, and put to work, they helped sustain the company through its struggles and raise it to a position of leadership in its industry and prominence in American business.

During the second period of IBM's development—from 1946 to the present—they have made it possible for us to take sweeping technological changes in stride and grow at a rate that has won IBM a place as one of the prime growth companies of the nation.

Let's take a look at this growth.

Within a period of two generations, we have expanded from an awkward combination of three small companies into an international company whose revenues in the United States and abroad exceeded $2 billion in 1961.

In 1914, when my father joined the company, its products consisted of butcher scales, meat slicers, coffee grinders, time clocks, and a primitive assortment of punched card tabulating machines. Today IBM computers are in the forefront of a new technology which some say will have a greater ultimate impact on society than any other invention of the past fifty years.

During the last forty-eight years, IBM has grown from a company of 1,200 people to one of more than 125,000—two-thirds of them in all fifty of the United States, the remainder in ninety-four countries overseas. Domestic revenues alone have increased more than 400 times over the $4 million a year the company grossed in 1914. Not once during those forty-seven years did the company fail to make a profit. Not since 1916 has it ever had to pass a cash dividend. In all, it has split its stock a total of eight times, five times during the last ten years. In addition, the company has declared twenty-five stock dividends.

During the same period, profits after taxes rose from about half a million to more than $200 million. The company had almost 800 stockholders in 1914;

today we have more than 225,000. If an individual had bought 100 shares of our stock in 1914, it would have cost him $2,750. And if he had left those shares untouched, they would have been worth $5,455,000 by September 30, 1962. One hundred shares, bought for $21,300 as late as 1950, would have been worth almost $333,000.

All this occurred in forty-eight years, about the working lifetime of most businessmen.

In appearance, IBM today is quite different from the company it was in 1920, 1930, or even in 1940. Its products have changed from tabulating machines with Queen Anne legs to high-powered computers, some of which can perform at the rate of more than 600,000 calculations per second. The starched collar is gone, along with our company songs, trade marks of the 1920s and '30s.

But in its attitude, its outlook, its spirit, its drive, IBM is still very much the same company it has always been and that we intend it shall always be. For while everything else has altered, our beliefs remain unchanged.

2

HELPING MEN GROW

The beliefs that mold great organizations frequently grow out of the character, the experiences, and the convictions of a single person. More than most companies, IBM is the reflection of one individual—my father, T. J. Watson.

Father joined the company at forty, a point at which most businessmen, thinking they were middle-aged, might not feel able to start a new career. He had, by that time, a firm grip on most of the beliefs he felt necessary to be successful in business. He held to them so strongly that he was sometimes exasperating. But the depth of his belief was directly related to the success of our company.

My father was the son of an upstate New York farmer. He grew up in an ordinary but happy home where the means, and perhaps the wants, were modest and the moral environment strict. The important values, as he learned them, were to do every job well, to treat all people with dignity and respect, to appear neatly dressed, to be clean and forthright, to be eternally optimistic, and above all, loyal.

There was nothing very unusual about this. It was a normal upbringing in rural nineteenth-century America. Whereas most men took the lessons of childhood for granted, however, and either lived by them or quietly forgot them, my father had the compulsion to work hard at them all his life. As far as he was concerned, those values were the rules of life—to be preserved at all costs, to be commended to others, and to be followed conscientiously in one's business life.

These early lessons were later reinforced by John H. Patterson, then president and major owner of The National Cash Register Company. Patterson was an eccentric in many ways, but he was a remarkable modern business pioneer—really a social reformer—as well as the father of modern salesmanship. His personality, his methods, and his liberal employee policies had a great impact on T. J. Watson. And my father was not alone in this. Patterson trained a number of outstanding businessmen who went on to notable success. Among them were Charles Kettering, the great inventor; Alvan Macauley, long-time head of Packard; and R. H. Grant, former president of Delco Light, and Frigidaire, and later sales vice-president of General Motors.

IBM's philosophy is largely contained in three simple beliefs.

I want to begin with what I think is the most important: *our respect for the individual*. This is a simple concept, but in IBM it occupies a major portion of management time. We devote more effort to it than anything else.

This belief was bone-deep in my father. Some people who start out in modest circumstances have a certain contempt for the average man when they are able to rise above him. Others, by the time they become leaders, have built up a unique respect and understanding for the average man and a sympathy for his problems. They recognize that in a modern industrial nation the less fortunate often are victims of forces not wholly within their own control. This attitude forms the basis for many of the decisions they make having to do with people. T. J. Watson was in the latter category. He had known hard times, hard work, and unemployment himself, and he always had understanding for the problems of the working man. Moreover, he recognized that the greatest of these problems was job security.

In 1914, having been fired as sales manager of National Cash following a series of clashes with Mr. Patterson, my father was brought in to run the Computing-Tabulating-Recording Company, a loose alliance of three small companies. It was the organization that was to become IBM ten years later.

C-T-R was a demoralized organization. Many of the people there resented the newcomer who had been brought into the organization and quarreled among themselves. It was a situation that presented him with an early test of his belief in job security.

14

Despite the questionable condition of the company, no one was fired. T. J. Watson didn't move in and shake up the organization. Instead he set out to buff and polish the people who were already there and to make a success of what he had.

That decision in 1914 led to the IBM policy on job security which has meant a great deal to our employees. From it has come our policy to build from within. We go to great lengths to develop our people, to retrain them when job requirements change, and to give them another chance if we find them experiencing difficulties in the jobs they are in.

This does not mean that a job at IBM is a lifetime ticket or that we do not occasionally let people go—we do, but only after we have made a genuine effort to help them improve. Nor does it mean that people do not leave us—they do. But policies like these, we have found, help us to win the good will of most of our people.

Among plant people, where job security is ordinarily a matter of major concern, IBM's ability to avoid layoffs and work interruptions has encouraged our people to respond with loyalty and with diligence on the job. Over the years we have been willing to take chances and strain our resources rather than resort to layoffs. For almost a quarter of a century now, no one has lost an hour's time in layoffs from IBM, in spite of recessions and major product shifts.

Fortunately we have had a relatively steady market, which has helped make this record possible. But there have been times when we might have taken the easy way out to save payroll. During the Great Depression, for example, when nearly one-quarter of the civilian labor force was unemployed, IBM embarked on a program of expansion. Rather than resort to mass factory layoffs, IBM produced parts for inventory and stored them. It was a gamble that took nerve, especially for a company doing less than $17 million worth of business a year. Happily, the risk paid off in 1935, when Congress passed the Social Security Act and IBM, in competitive bidding, was selected to undertake one of the greatest bookkeeping operations of all time. Thanks to our stockpiling of parts, we were able to build the machines and begin delivery almost at once.

Today our frequent attitude surveys show that the importance we attach to job security is one of

16

the principal reasons why people like to work for IBM.

Steady employment, however, is only one part of good human relations, an area where IBM inherited much from John Patterson. In many ways Patterson was a typical nineteenth-century businessman. He deplored competition and went to great lengths to overcome it. On the other hand, while most businessmen were fighting off the demands of their workers, Patterson made great strides in employee welfare. He was decades ahead of his time. Early in his career he had learned a hard lesson when indifferent workmen produced $50,000 worth of defective machines and almost ruined his company. Patterson's response was to build modern factories with improved facilities for his people. He provided showers on company premises and company time, dining rooms serving meals at cost, entertainment, schools, clubs, libraries, and parks. Other businessmen were shocked at Patterson's notions. But he said they were investments which would pay off—and they did. T. J. Watson observed Patterson's practices carefully and carried many of them with him to IBM.

In the early days C-T-R was working so close to the line that there was no money available to duplicate Patterson's handsome factory buildings and his generous benefits programs. Father used showmanship instead. He staged band concerts and picnics and made scores of speeches. Almost every kind of fanfare was tried to create enthusiasm. The more substantial things—above-average wages and benefits—came later.

Along with wages and job security, we have always thought it equally important that the company respect the dignity of its employees. People, as I have said, occupy more IBM management time than our products. As businessmen we think in terms of profits, but people continue to rank first. Occasionally our actions have been harsh. Sometimes a fair amount of dignity has been stripped from individual managers who were being ineffective, but great efforts were then made to rebuild their pride so they could carry on with self-respect.

Our early emphasis on human relations was not motivated by altruism but by the simple belief that if we respected our people and helped them to respect themselves the company would make the most profit.

Our management also recognized that the individual has his own problems, ambitions, abilities, frustrations, and goals. We wanted to be certain that no one got lost in the organization and, most of all, that no individual became a victim of any manager's unfairness or personal whim. In this regard, we developed what we call our "Open Door" policy. This is a key element in our employee relations.

The Open Door grew out of T. J. Watson's close and frequent association with individuals in the plant and field offices. It became a natural thing for them to bring their problems to him and in time was established as a regular procedure. My father encouraged this in his visits. He spoke of it in his telephone broadcasts to offices and plants. If a man was not getting along, or if he thought he was being treated unfairly by his manager, he was told to go to the plant or branch manager. If that did not work, he was then invited to come and lay his case before my father.

Hundreds of employees literally did just that.

Many would take the day off from our plant in Endicott, N. Y., and come to his office in New York City to talk about their problems. More often than not, he favored the complaining employee—sometimes, I'm sure, more than he should have. But he built up a lasting relationship with a great many employees and they helped him to keep in touch with what was going on in the company. At the time of his death in 1956, most of our then 57,000 employees thought of T. J. Watson as a friend they could count on.

The Open Door exists today as it did then. I'm sure that a policy of this kind makes many a traditional manager's blood run cold. He probably sees it as a challenge to his authority or, worse yet, as a sharp sword hanging over his head. But the fact remains that in IBM it has been remarkably effective, primarily because—by its mere existence—it exercises a moderating influence on management. Whenever a manager makes a decision affecting one of his people, he knows that he may be held accountable to higher management for the fairness of that decision.

From time to time we have had second thoughts

on the practicality of this policy, especially now that IBM has grown to a company of over 80,000 people in the United States alone. Obviously, if everyone with a problem insisted on seeing the president or me, we would both have run out of time long ago.

The answer, in the future, may have to come in a shift downward in this court of appeal, possibly to the level of division president or general manager. But whatever the difficulties, we certainly have no intention of denying anyone the opportunity to talk to whomever he wishes to in this business. Whether they exercise it or not, our people are reassured by the fact that they have this right. And by its existence, I believe, it acts as a deterrent to the possible abuse of managerial power.

Our management has long believed that sharp contrast between the blue- and the white-collar people in a business is to be avoided. For many years IBM benefits were the same for all employees with a given amount of service, regardless of rank or position. Insurance and vacation programs to this day relate to service. Other benefits, such as medical care, are the same for all. In our retirement plan, however, we now recognize salary as well as length of service.

Years ago all piecework was eliminated in our plants. First-line managers in the plants did not keep data on the production of parts because we did not want their evaluation of workers directly related to units produced. The IBM employee was compensated on the basis of his manager's judgment of his overall contribution to the business.

Obviously some of these practices caused inefficiencies. Yet on the whole they contributed in a major way to the morale of the hourly rated man.

Naturally the key factor in the maintenance of good human relations is the individual manager, and when my father first went on the road for The National Cash Register Company, he learned a lesson in management that he made a permanent part of IBM. Right after he joined "The Cash" as it was known, he spent several weeks calling on prospects without making a single sale. His manager had him on the carpet, and after treating him pretty roughly, he said: "Young man, I'll go out with you when you call on your prospects, and if we fall down we'll fall down together." They went out and together made several sales. After that, having learned a little more about how to sell and after having recaptured his confidence, T. J. Watson found the job a great deal easier. The episode made a tremendous impression on him.

Today this same approach is expected of all IBM managers. The manager must know how to work with his people, how to help them, and how to train them. For example, if a salesman is having difficulty, we insist that his branch manager or even his district manager make a number of calls with him to help him improve.

Another consideration in human relations that has meant a great deal is the continual opportunity for advancement. Because we have grown so rapidly, we have created a great many opportunities for promotion. No matter how great the temptation to go outside for managers, we have almost always filled these new jobs from within; no more than a small percentage of our people have come into the company other than at the lowest level in their specialty. We have hired a few top scientists, lawyers, and other specialists, but with those exceptions all our executives came up from the bottom. This has been a great factor in maintaining morale.

You cannot always make as many promotions in a plant as you can elsewhere, but we have found that there are other things you can do to keep morale high. One technique is job enlargement. People running a nearly automatic machine tool all day making hundreds of the same item may have very little feeling of personal accomplishment. In IBM we fight this problem whenever practical by teaching our people to do their own set-up work when they change from one operation to another. In some cases they make up unit assemblies. In others, they do their own inspecting. We try to rotate the very boring jobs to break monotony. This helps a person to keep his sense of dignity, accomplishment, and involvement.

Cause and effect are often impossible to match up, but I have always been convinced that without our attitude toward human relations we would have fallen short of our business goals.

Some say that when an organization tries to get too close to its people and makes a lot of the "team"

idea, the individual get swallowed up, loses his identity, and becomes a carbon copy of his fellow employees. So far as I can see, this is not true to any
serious degree in our large organizations today. Corporate people may not necessarily be more inde-
pendent than others, but neither do I believe that
they are any less.

I suspect we have our fair quota of security-
minded men who are careful never to rock the boat.
At the same time I suspect there are some college
professors who are absent-minded, some scientists
who are eccentric, and some military men who are
martinets. But just as these stereotypes do not apply
to the general run of people in those occupations,
the stereotype of the "organization man" does not
apply to all forms of corporate life.

IBM has more than 125,000 employees. A substantial number of them, many of whom I could
pick out by name, are highly individualistic men and
women. They value their social and intellectual freedom, and I question whether they would surrender
it at any price. Admittedly, they may like their jobs
and the security and salaries that go along with
them. But I know of few who would not put on their

hats and slam the door if they felt the organization had intruded so heavily on them that they no longer owned themselves. Business may have its share of hypocrites, but I am sure that big business has no more than any other group.

Early in 1961, in talking to our sales force, I attempted to size up the then new Kennedy Administration as I saw it. It was not a political talk. I urged no views on them. It was an optimistic assessment, nothing more. But at the close of the meeting, a number of salesmen came up front. They would listen to what I had to say about business, they said, but they didn't want to hear about the new Administration in a company meeting.

On my return to New York, I found a few letters in the same vein. Lay off, they seemed to say, you're stepping on our toes in something that's none of your business.

At first I was a bit annoyed at having been misunderstood. But when I thought about it, I was pleased, for they had made it quite clear they wore no man's collar and they weren't at all hesitant to tell me so. From what I have read of organization men, that is not the way they are supposed to act.

It is interesting to contemplate the possible nature of individual achievement in the absence of large organizations. It probably would be of a different order. The challenges in a large organization are great, and achievement, really, is the successful response to challenge. Men who have accomplished great deeds in large organizations might have done less if they had been challenged with less, and they would have realized less of their potential and their individuality.

In IBM we frequently refer to our need for "wild ducks." The moral is drawn from a story by the Danish philosopher, Soren Kierkegård. He told of a man on the coast of Zealand who liked to watch the wild ducks fly south in great flocks each fall. Out of charity, he took to putting feed for them in a nearby pond. After a while some of the ducks no longer bothered to fly south; they wintered in Denmark on what he fed them.

In time they flew less and less. When the wild ducks returned, the others would circle up to greet them but then head back to their feeding grounds on the pond. After three or four years they grew so lazy and fat that they found difficulty in flying at all.

27

Kierkegård drew his point—you can make wild ducks tame, but you can never make tame ducks wild again. One might also add that the duck who is tamed will never go anywhere any more.

We are convinced that any business needs its wild ducks. And in IBM we try not to tame them.

3

SERVICE AND SUPERIORITY

Years ago we ran an ad that said simply and in bold type, "IBM Means Service." I have often thought it our very best ad. It stated clearly just exactly what we stand for. It also is a succinct expression of our second basic corporate belief. *We want to give the best customer service of any company in the world.*

We recognize that service is the key element in what I hope is our good reputation. T. J. Watson realized early the great importance of reputation. When he was eighteen he drove a horse and buggy across northern New York State selling pianos and sewing machines. His customers were farmers and, like farmers everywhere at the time, they seldom had much cash. To make a sale he frequently took animals or farm equipment in trade, later selling them off in Painted Post, his home base. He had two years of good training in how to get along with people, how to make a fair trade and leave people happy. As he drove his team through the countryside the second time he saw at once the value of the Golden Rule in business, for many people would buy his goods on the basis of what satisfied customers had to say about his products.

IBM's sales and service forces bear the prime responsibility for our rigid insistence on service. To maintain our reputation for excellent service, we long ago established high standards for the selection of salesmen and customer engineers.

To attract top-quality salesmen, IBM used sales commissions, advances, quotas, and guaranteed territories, at a time when most of those practices were still looked upon as innovations. Schools were set up for salesmen—the training course now runs as long as eighteen months—and we began to visit colleges to recruit our sales trainees.

Equal care was taken in the selection and training of customer engineers. With high-speed electronic equipment and large systems installations, the job requirements have since become so demanding that we interview an average of twenty-five applicants for each one we hire.

In its commitment to customer service, IBM learned that the best way to serve a prospect was to provide equipment adapted to his requirements, rather than ask him to alter his business to fit our machines.

We found that good service to the customer requires the cooperation of all parts of the business. I think this was brought home to us years ago when we centered many of our activities on our plant in Endicott. Sales and customer engineering schools were located there, as were our sales conventions in the 1940s. Customer executives and administrative personnel also visited and studied at Endicott. This arrangement brought together all our people, as well as our customers, and made it possible for us to give the latter better service as we learned more about their problems.

In a business like ours, a reputation for service is

one of the company's principal assets. Many operations performed by our machines are vital to the customer's business. Lengthy breakdowns could be ruinous. Furthermore, most of what we call "sales" in IBM are really rentals. IBM's contracts have always offered, not machines for rent, but machine services, that is the equipment itself and the continuing advice and counsel of IBM's staff.

In the normal course of business we will do everything possible to maintain our reputation for service. On the rare occasion when a new installation gets into trouble as the result of a changeover in procedures, or when a system is damaged by fire or flood, our customer engineers, sales and systems staffs think nothing of nursing the system through long nights and weekends. More than one branch manager has worked overnight in his shirtsleeves to help get a customer's salary checks out on time.

In time, good service became almost a reflex in IBM, and father loved to show what the company could do. In 1942 an official of the War Production Board gave him a perfect excuse to do it. The WPB man called him late on the afternoon of Good Friday to place an order for 150 machines, challenging him to deliver the equipment by the following Monday in Washington, D. C. Father said he would have the machines there on time. On Saturday morning, he and his staff phoned IBM offices all over the country and instructed them to get some 150 machines on the road that Easter weekend. Just to make sure his caller got the point, father instructed his staff to wire the WPB man at his office or home the minute each truck started on its way to Washington, giving the time of departure and expected arrival. He made arrangements with police and Army officials to escort the trucks which were to be driven around the clock. Customer engineers were brought in and a miniature factory set up in Georgetown to handle the reception and installation of the equipment. There were sleepless people in IBM—and in WPB—that weekend.

These are not small things. The relationship between the man and the customer, their mutual trust, the importance of reputation, the idea of putting the customer first—always—all these things, if carried out with real conviction by a company, can make a great deal of difference in its destiny.

The third IBM belief is really the force that makes the other two effective. *We believe that an organization should pursue all tasks with the idea that they can be accomplished in a superior fashion.* IBM expects and demands superior performance from its people in whatever they do.

I suppose a belief of this kind conjures up a mania for perfection and all the psychological horrors that go with it. Admittedly, a perfectionist is seldom a comfortable personality. An environment which calls for perfection is not likely to be easy. But aiming for it is always a goad to progress.

In addition to this persistent striving for perfection, we believe an organization will stand out only if it is willing to take on seemingly impossible tasks. The men who set out to do what others say cannot be done are the ones who make the discoveries, produce the inventions, and move the world ahead.

T. J. Watson used to tell our people, "It is better to aim at perfection and miss than it is to aim at imperfection and hit it."

As a result of this insistence on perfection and the way we went at almost impossible tasks, there soon developed within the company what might best be called a *tone*. It was a blend of optimism, enthusiasm, excitement, and pace. The company was always on the move, constantly changing, always striving for something better. Evidences of it were everywhere—new products, new branch offices, sales contests, slogans. Better to do something—even the wrong thing—than to do nothing at all.

Believing in success can help to make it so. Back in 1924 when things like butcher scales and time clocks were still mainstays of our business we had the temerity to change our name from the Computing-Tabulating-Recording Company to the International Business Machines Corporation. We constantly acted as though we were much bigger, much more sophisticated, much more successful than any current balance sheet might bear out.

As I have already pointed out, part of this tone was optimism, of course, and in this my father excelled. One day during the Depression of the thirties, my father met one of his major competitors in an art gallery. IBM was not doing particularly well but was managing to equal its previous year's income. The other fellow was having more difficulty.

He said to my father: "Tom, I hear you're still

hiring salesmen in spite of the Depression, and I just can't see how that's a prudent thing for your business."

My father said: "Well, Bill, you know when a man gets about my age, he always does something foolish. Some men play too much poker, and others bet on horse races, and one thing and another. My hobby is hiring salesmen."

This optimism, which may have been little more than an enlightened guess, paid off. When business turned up the next year and then started to boom during and after the war, IBM was awfully glad my father had hired those salesmen.

We had an IBM day at the World's Fair of 1939, and next year brought 10,000 of our people to the Fair at company expense. People realized they were working for an unusual individual and an unusual company that was capable of doing unusual things.

By the 1930s our sales conventions had become spectacular affairs. Salesmen, on awakening, would find newspapers under their doors carrying a complete account of the previous day's events. Our overseas salesmen attended our conventions at that time, and when they got to their seats, they found small headphones with which they could hear the speeches in their native tongues.

When General Eisenhower, then president of Columbia University, went to Endicott to address a Hundred Percent Club meeting in July, 1948, T. J. Watson persuaded him to spend an extra hour and talk to the plant people. Within that same hour the people were let off from their jobs and a platform was constructed in the street outside the main plant. As the General and my father climbed the steps, the carpenters hammered in the last nails. "My gosh," one worker was heard to say, "what a business."

In a way, no one knew quite what to expect next. It may not have been management according to the book, but it seemed to keep us on our toes. Things were always being done in a highly vigorous fashion, with little regard for how much energy was being expended, but with a great regard for the quality of the result and for the impression it would make on people.

In 1934 we told the sales force that as soon as the company's profits were doubled the annual convention would be held in Europe. All salesmen making their quotas would qualify for the trip. The year of doubled profits came in 1941, but Hitler had other plans for Europe, and the idea of the trip was swallowed up by the war. Then in 1961 one of our old-timers, a salesman who had qualified for that trip, wrote to remind me that the pledge had never been fulfilled. I knew that I had to make good on the promise and was glad of the opportunity. So in the summer of 1962, 187 salesmen who had qualified for that trip traveled to Europe with their wives to keep the date that had been interrupted.

The trip provided an interchange between American and European salesmen with, we hope, mutual benefits. In addition, it proved to be a great morale-booster on both sides of the ocean.

Looking back on it now, I can see that many of the things we did in the formative years were anything but scientific. But what we learned, I believe, is that there are times in an organization when an instinct for leadership and drama are many times more important than following the book on good management procedure.

What T. J. Watson did, probably more than anything else, was to set the tone for IBM. This was created in large part by the beliefs he brought to the company, for with them he brought vigor and great excitement. But it was also colored by his own good sense of what would be the most appropriate for the time and the situation. When things were difficult and the sledding was uphill, he could be very optimistic. But when things looked good and our future began to clear up, he was forever cautioning us against getting complacent about it. I suspect this is a necessity for any leader—to be a balance wheel, a leavener.

Certainly no one can argue with the results. From 1914 to 1946 our company's profits grew thirty-eight times. By the end of World War II, IBM's management had developed a deep belief in the policies upon which we had built our business: respect for the individual, major attention to service, drive for superiority in all things.

Undoubtedly the principal reason these beliefs have worked well is that they fit together and support one another. If you hire good people and treat them well, they will try to do a good job. They will stimulate one another by their vigor and example.

They will set a fast pace for themselves. Then, if they are well led and occasionally inspired, if they understand what the company is trying to do and know they will share in its success, they will contribute in a major way. The customer will get the superior service he is looking for. The result is profit to customers, employees, and stockholders.

I know some people believe our approach to business is a luxury that can be indulged in only because of the nature of our operation and the excellent profit it makes. We certainly would not have been as successful in a less promising field. But I believe very deeply that whatever business we might have been in, given the same beliefs and the same early leadership, we still would have been out in front.

It is interesting to note that we didn't have quite the clear sailing that some people seem to think we had in our industry. When Dr. Herman Hollerith was developing the original electrically sensed punched card, there was another engineer with him in the Census Bureau by the name of James Powers. Powers took out patents on a mechanically sensed punched card that gave about the same results as ours.

Service and Superiority

The Powers patents have been in the hands of reputable companies for as long as the Hollerith patents have been in ours. In fact holders of those patents have produced a number of firsts in our industry—including the first printing tabulating machine and the first alphabetic printer. Each time we are second-best in a new machine announcement, we take it as a personal affront and redouble our efforts to be more responsive to customers' needs.

Occasionally we have failed to respond with vigor, and when this has happened we have always lost ground. When we lost ground to others in those areas in which we have competence, we did so because we forgot to strive for superiority. This is easy to do when you are generally successful. "Well, you can't win them all," you just say, "and the overall picture is good." This is the first step towards failure. We've taken it once or twice, but fortunately we've never failed to correct our mistakes before they became a habit.

4

THE NEW ENVIRONMENT

IBM came out of World War II a large corporation, the largest in our industry.

During those first thirty-two years between 1914 and 1946 we had tested and put to work our strong corporate beliefs. Now we were to be faced with the task of adhering to those beliefs while the organization—as well as the world around it—faced new challenges and changed radically to meet them.

In the maintenance of our beliefs through change we were to experience problems vastly different from those we had known before. It was one thing to adhere to our beliefs when we were a relatively small company with only a few thousand employees, a company where the product line shifted slowly over the years and which was run, essentially, by a few executives. It was another to live by those same beliefs through a tumult of change which was to bring with it new techniques, new products, new markets, and a staggering increase in the company's size.

First, there was the matter of growth alone. From domestic gross revenues of $115 million in 1946 IBM went on to increase them by a factor of fourteen, until in 1961 they stood at $1.7 billion. Employees in the United States went from 17,000 to almost 80,000. During these same fifteen postwar years our data processing customers grew from 6,000 to 19,000. On the manufacturing side, we had been largely a New York State company, with major plants in Endicott and Poughkeepsie. Since 1950, we have built eleven new plants in nine states—all the way from Vermont to California.

In 1946 our overseas operations were relatively small. They were run as a department of the domestic company. Last year the many companies that make up our wholly owned IBM World Trade Corporation had a gross revenue of just under half a billion dollars. This was in addition to our $1.7 billion of domestic revenue. From West Berlin, where a new IBM office has just been completed, to Bangkok, where an IBM installation is housed in the royal palace, IBM World Trade is growing at a rate faster than that of the domestic company.

In technology, too, we have experienced vast changes. Before the war there were many major similarities between our machines of 1918 and those of 1938. To be sure, there were more of them and their capacities had been increased, but they operated very much in the same way and on the same old principle of the electrically sensed punched card. Now the equipment is changing so rapidly that a substantial part of our data processing revenues comes from machines announced only six years before. Whole new generations of electronic computers come along in rapid order.

The shift from electromechanical punched card equipment to electronic computers with magnetic tape inputs and high-speed printers was as revolutionary, in its way, as the advance in the aerospace industry from DC-3s to Titan missiles. These changes had a wide-sweeping effect on our people and on everything they did. To design and build the new computers, we had to create large engineering and technical forces and retrain many of our production people. To sell the new systems and put them to work, we had to expand and retrain our sales staff. We helped to create whole new professions, such as programming and systems engineering. And to install and maintain the equipment, we had to recruit and train a nationwide force of skilled customer engineers.

In the 1930s the engineering people we hired had conventional electrical or mechanical training. Now we had to look for scores of new disciplines—many of them in critically short supply. Our laboratories began to fill up with specialists in areas of electronics and physics, with chemists, metallurgists, and mathematicians. Our operations now demanded basic research in a number of important areas. We went heavily into applied research and engineering. We needed theoretical thinking of the highest order.

These changes had profound effects on our operations in the field. Salesmen trained to market relatively simple accounting machines suddenly found themselves responsible for enormously complex million-dollar computer installations. Customer engineers entered a strange new world of electronic testing equipment.

The magnitude of this changeover can probably best be illustrated by the advances that have been made in computing speeds during the last two decades. The first large-scale computer, the Mark I, built by IBM in collaboration with Dr. Howard Aiken and presented to Harvard University in 1944, was capable of three calculations per second. The first commercially available large-scale IBM computer, the 701, in 1952 did 16,000 a second. Today machines capable of more than 225,000 calculations a second are commonplace in the industry.

Other features of the data processing operations have also been speeded up. Punched cards used to enter data into the machines at the rate of 133 characters a second; now magnetic tape can feed data into computers at the rate of 170,000 characters a second.

These concurrent explosions in technology and growth put severe strains on our organization, but I think we have come through them with a reasonable degree of success. There were many problems, to be sure, and most of them were new to us. Some we have solved, others are still with us, but in almost every case we've learned some hard lessons along the way. And many of them have to do with our beliefs.

During the period prior to 1946 it was quite easy for us to make everyone understand how interested we were in the well-being of our people. For one thing we had relatively few of them. For another, we added to them slowly. When a man joined the company he would, in time, learn of its traditions from his manager and others with whom he worked.

But with the rapid changes that began to take place as a result of technology and growth in the years following 1946, we found it harder to convince the individual employee that we still looked upon him as the most important asset in the corporation.

Prior to 1946 our sales growth rate averaged more than 12 per cent a year. During the early 1950s we grew at the rate of 24 per cent a year. If the company's beliefs were to count for anything, we would have to make it very clear to new employees what IBM stood for.

Naturally we had recourse to all the usual company communications. But the key to helping our people understand lay with the individual managers. Unfortunately, most of our managers in the middle and later 1950s had been with the company a very short time, and it was difficult for them to explain our traditional philosophies.

We attacked the problem by setting up two management schools—one for junior executives, another two years later for line managers. These schools were not only to teach general management, but—most important—they were to give our managers a feeling for IBM's outlook and its beliefs. After a time we found that the schools tended to put too much emphasis on management, not enough on the beliefs. This, we felt, was putting the cart before the horse, so we changed the curriculum. We felt it was vital that our managers be well grounded in our beliefs. Otherwise, we might begin to get management views at odds with the company's outlook. If this were to happen, it might possibly slow down our growth and change our basic approach to the management of our company.

But even assuming that the individual manager has been soundly grounded in IBM's beliefs, there is always the possibility that the pressure of his job may cause him to compromise them. This is a natural tendency, I suppose, especially for the manager rated on the profitability of his operation. At what point, for example, does the pressure he puts on employees begin to violate the company's belief in respect for the individual? In 1956 we reorganized the company into divisions and started to emphasize profit as the measure of each division's performance. At that point we began to see clearly that some division managers might become so profit-minded that they would lose track of our beliefs unless constantly reminded by top management.

In one instance our customer engineers were spread too thinly across customer installations. This was good for profit, but the morale of the overworked customer engineers began to sag. Our high standards of service were certainly in jeopardy. Corners had been cut on two beliefs—respect for the individual and service to the customers. We quickly righted the imbalance and looked for other ways to hold the cost line.

While the beliefs may be clear enough, practicing them is not always a matter of course. For example, for years we had operated our plants on the basis of a fair day's work for a fair day's pay, no piecework, no individual daily quotas. This practice proved a great shot in the arm when the company needed it most—in its early years when morale was being built. But later, injustices crept in. I first got wind of what was happening when a young man came down from our Poughkeepsie plant to make use of the Open Door and tell me he thought he had been fired unfairly.

He had complained to his manager that although he was one of the highest producers in his department he was drawing one of the lowest wage rates. When his manager gave him no satisfaction, he went to the plant superintendent.

The latter listened and then replied, "It sounds to me as if you don't have any faith in the management of this plant."

"You're darned right," the young man said, "I don't."

The superintendent fired him on the spot.

When I looked into the situation I found that the young man was justified in his complaint—and there were probably others in the same fix. For what constitutes "a fair day's work" may mean one thing to one manager, another to the manager in the next department. In some instances low performers had climbed to the top of the pay scale, primarily because of their attitude and appearance. In others, high performers found themselves at the bottom of the scale. This was obviously unfair. What had started out as a program to raise morale had been changed so much by intermediate management that morale was actually lowered.

At the same time we found ourselves in an increasingly competitive situation, making it necessary for us to improve production and cut costs. To do this, we had to give managers bench marks against which they could measure performance. We began to introduce new techniques for the measurement of performance. Since we were still in a semi-inflationary period, it was possible to slow down raises for the low producers and speed them up for the high producers so as to correct the imbalance in pay-production ratio.

Traditionally IBM had been opposed to such things as time and motion studies, so when we decided to introduce some of these procedures the change had to be carefully planned. In some IBM divisions and plants the job was well done. In others, unimaginative managers took the attitude—"Well, it's a new and tough regime; you had better shape up or ship out." I began to get an increase in complaint letters and Open Door visits from our plant employees.

Many of these complaints were justified, for in many instances our people were irked. We learned a lot about some of our managers and employees as a result of these difficulties. Where necessary, the pressure was eased.

The problem is by no means entirely solved, but we feel that most people are now working in a more productive atmosphere. Morale improved, and this improvement enabled us to cut costs with less strain.

The mistake was the same one we had made in the instance of the customer engineers—we had let some managers in their zeal override human relations. As long as new programs of this kind are properly explained, there's seldom any trouble. Try to do it without sufficient explanation or without selling the idea, and you usually have trouble.

Although we might be said to have gone conventional on this matter of work measurement, we went off in the other direction on our compensation plan in 1958. In that year we eliminated the hourly wage and put everyone in IBM on straight salary. That move eliminated what had been the last distinction between our blue- and white-collar employees. I think this has meant as much to our people as any innovation we've made in human relations since the end of World War II.

On the question of fair treatment, I'm reminded of the lesson we learned about the transfers of our people in the field. With nearly two hundred branch offices and rapid company growth, a certain amount of moving was inevitable. But when people began to say that IBM stood for "I've Been Moved," we naturally looked into what we were doing in that area.

We found that many of these moves were really being made for the convenience of the company rather than for the benefit of the employee. This called for a new set of requirements, the principal one of which made it mandatory that a person moved on individual reassignment be given a substantial increase in responsibility and pay. This change resulted in relatively fewer moves. To make certain we were fair to those being moved, we introduced an improved program to minimize the individual's out-of-pocket moving costs.

In all good human relations communication plays a very important part. People can be directed, but they respond best when they understand what they are supposed to do and why. Until there is understanding, there is no real basis for motivation. I believe management must seek consent.

Our problems here have been pressing. From 1946 through 1962, IBM's worldwide population increased by more than 100,000 people. We are more spread out than ever. Growth has brought with it thousands of new managers. Despite our efforts to contain them, there are many new levels of management. We have had to face the problem of how to implant and keep alive in these people a real feeling for the traditions and beliefs of the business,

—how to keep them pulling together despite their natural diversity in interests,
—how to shorten the distance between the man at the bench and his division manager, the president, or the board chairman,

—how to maintain the "small company attitude" that meant so much to us at the time we were growing up.

This small company attitude is a term we frequently use. We encourage it in every way we can. We want our people to feel that they understand one another, that they have some knowledge of each other's problems and goals. And we want them to feel that they always have access to management, that no one is so far down in the chain of command that he cannot be kept aware of what is going on.

In IBM today there are eight levels of management between the man at the bench and the president or the board chairman. There are seven levels above the salesman. This is more than we like, but we try to keep it down to that. And we do a number of things to help shorten the distance.

Some are conventional. For example, we have a question and answer program that draws some 300 inquiries or complaints a month, and few of them pull their punches. We have a suggestion award program that brings in more than 100,000 entries a year; annual employee appraisals and frequent attitude surveys; and eighteen plant, division, and company news publications.

Others are more unusual. One is a newsletter called *Management Briefing.* A few years ago we surveyed a group of managers and found we were falling far short of keeping them well informed. Today *Management Briefing* goes regularly to more than 10,000 managers—the majority of whom many companies would call foremen.

Management Briefing provides our managers with background information on company announcements and activities. It explains the "why" behind policies, and it covers actual case studies—or object lessons—in management to help us avoid making the same mistake twice.

For communications to executives on very important matters, we began three years ago to issue "President's Letters"—they are now called "Executive Letters." On the average we publish fewer than a dozen a year, and they are used to explain basic IBM policies when we feel that such explanation is in order.

One of our most unique customs is the IBM Family Dinner. At least once every two years in every one of our branch offices around the country our people—along with their husbands or wives—are asked to dinner with an officer of the corporation to learn what is going on. In telling his story he shows a half-hour filmed report on what the company has done in the past year. These Family Dinners keep our executives on the go, but they give us an occasion where we can get together informally, and they help keep our small company attitude alive.

We also write letters of congratulations on promotions and jobs well done. And when our people get sick, or when they lose a member of their family, we remember them with notes of sympathy or condolence.

When I have an important announcement to make I do it by a telephone broadcast, very often to all our domestic employees. I believe it means more to them when they hear these announcements directly from me. There are seldom more than one or two a year—we save them for things that personally affect most of our people.

Quite aside from these usual communication problems, there is one area in particular where we

make a special effort to see that there is good understanding between management and our people. This
is in the whole area of business ethics and the ob-
servance of antitrust laws—specifically in compliance
with our consent decree.

About ten years ago we in IBM were considerably
disillusioned to learn of some shoddy practices in
purchasing. We had heard, of course, of such situa-
tions in other companies but thought it could never
happen to us. We promptly and vigorously cor-
rected the situation.

This breakdown, however, reminded us that
people, after all, are people and that bringing them
into IBM doesn't put any magic, protective cloak
around them. To keep a company ethical and clean
is the responsibility of top management. It can never
be left to chance.

With all of these innovations we have introduced
in company communication, the principal lesson we
have learned, I believe, is that you must make use of
a number of pipelines, upward as well as downward.
Parallel communication paths may seem unnecessary to some. But we have found that any single
path can be only partly successful, that certain in-

formation flows better over some paths than others, and that all employees do not react in the same way to a given medium. Management must have a wide selection of communication means at its disposal. And, probably even more important, the employee must have a variety of ways through which he can make his voice heard by management.

But before leaving this whole question of attitudes and communication there is one point on which I have some real concern. It has to do with the cautious attitude of so many young men in middle management today. They seem reluctant to stick their necks out or to bet on a hunch.

This is not always because they lack nerve. Sometimes they make the mistake of thinking that top management places a greater premium on following form than on anything else. I wish we could stir them up a bit and encourage a little more recklessness among this group of decision makers. Every time we've moved ahead in IBM, it was because someone was willing to take a chance, put his head on the block, and try something new.

5

WHAT GROWTH AND CHANGE
HAVE TAUGHT US

I said earlier that the great technological changes
we have been going through have had a sweeping
effect on our company. These changes have demanded a great deal of adaptability and versatility
from our employees.

We have learned that a company must be prepared to make a commitment to internal education
and retraining which increases in geometric proportion to the technological change the company is
going through.

During the 1962 session of Congress the Federal government assumed broad responsibilities for a retraining program. This program is aimed particularly at the jobless work force. It was a constructive move, and one which was probably overdue. But it in no way relieves corporations of the responsibilities they bear for the retraining of their own people. When skill requirements change, it is the job of the corporation to train its people in those new skills. A good many are already doing so. Those that are not, ought to. It would be wrong for businessmen to use the Federal retraining program as a substitute for one of their own.

Our own manufacturing changed drastically as we moved from electromechanical to electronic assembly. The changeover came with great speed and cut deeply into almost everything we were doing. Our plant in Poughkeepsie, New York, is a good example, for during the war we made weapons there. Then it converted to the manufacture of electromechanical equipment—chiefly typewriters and punched card accounting machines. Along came the computer, and the plant had to shift into electronics —first vacuum tubes and later transistors. Every-

where we turned, there were new problems in manufacture, new problems in automated assembly. In
all, we had about 6,000 manufacturing people who
were directly affected—not only production workers,
but managers as well.

The job is not over and, in all likelihood, never
will be. For as soon as one generation of computers
goes on the line, another is taking shape in the development laboratory. Some IBM departments may
have as many as one-quarter of their people in retraining at one time.

This commitment to education and retraining is
just as great in our marketing organization as it is
elsewhere. For our salesmen, this business of school
has become an everyday thing. And in our service
group, customer engineers must constantly update
themselves and learn new skills.

Technological change demands an even greater
measure of adaptability and versatility on the part
of management in a large organization. Unless management remains alert, it can be stricken with complacency—one of the most insidious dangers we face
in business. In most cases it's hard to tell that you've

even caught the disease until it's almost too late. It is frequently most infectious among companies that have already reached the top. They get to believing in the infallibility of their own judgments.

We had a bout with this disease soon after the war. It had to do with the introduction of the electronic computer—one of the most important single developments in the whole history of our industry. During the late 1940s it had become clear that many large engineering jobs and a good many accounting applications were being hampered by the relatively slow speeds of the calculating machines then available. At about that time J. Presper Eckert and Dr. John W. Mauchly of the Moore School at the University of Pennsylvania had built for the Army a large electronic computer—the Eniac—to make ballistic-curve calculations. Many people in our industry, and I was among them, had seen the machine, but none of us foresaw its possibilities. Even after Eckert and Mauchly left teaching to begin manufacture of a civilian counterpart to the Eniac, few of us saw the potential.

Their company was absorbed by Remington

Rand in 1950, and the following year the first production model of Univac was delivered to the
Census Bureau, where it replaced some IBM
machines.

Throughout this entire period IBM was unaware
of the fact that its whole business stood on the
threshold of a momentous change. We had put the
first electronically operated punched card calculator
on the market in 1946. Even in those days we were
well aware that electronic computing was so fast
that the machine waited nine-tenths of the time of
every card cycle for the mechanical parts of the
machine to feed the next card. Yet in spite of this
we didn't jump to the obvious conclusion that if
we could feed data faster we would increase com-
putational speeds 900 per cent. Remington Rand
had seen just that—and with Univac they were off to
the races.

The loss of our business in the Census Bureau
struck home. We began to act. We took one of our
best operating executives, a man with a reputation
for getting things done, and put him in charge of
everything which had to do with the introduction
of an IBM large-scale computer—all the way from

design and development through to marketing and servicing. He was so successful that within a short time we were well on our way.

How did we come up from behind so fast? First, we had enough cash to carry the costs of engineering, research, and production. Second, we had a sales force whose knowledge of the market enabled us to tailor our machines very closely to the needs. Finally, and most important, we had good company morale. Everyone realized that this was a challenge to our leadership. We had to respond with everything we had—and we did.

By 1956 it had become clear that in order for us to move rapidly with these technological changes we needed a new organization concept. Prior to the mid-1950s the company was run essentially by one man, T. J. Watson. He had a terrific team around him, but it was he who made the decisions. Had IBM had an organization chart at that time, there would have been a fascinating number of lines—perhaps thirty in all—running into his office.

In the early 1950s the demands of an expanding economy and the Korean War made it necessary for

IBM to react more rapidly at all levels than we were able to with our monolithic structure. Increasing customer pressure—to say nothing of a few missteps like the one we made on the electronic computer— caused us to decide on a new and greatly decentralized organization.

We wasted no time in carrying our decision out. In late 1956, after several months of planning, we called the top 100 or so people in the business to a three-day meeting at Williamsburg, Virginia. We went into that meeting a top-heavy, monolithic company and came out of it decentralized.

Today we have eight operating divisions and two wholly owned, but independently operated, subsidiaries. All have a considerable degree of autonomy. Sitting over them and reviewing their long-range plans and major decisions is the Corporate Management Committee, made up of the board chairman, the president, and six other top executives. Available to advise both this committee and the divisions is a corporate staff of specialists in such areas as manufacturing, engineering, personnel, finance, communications, law, and marketing.

We decentralized in more or less the usual way

and for the usual reasons—that is, to divide the business into more manageable units and to make sure that decisions would be made where and when they should be.

But in one respect we were quite different from most other companies. IBM is not the kind of business that textbooks say can be decentralized sensibly. We are not, as many large companies are, a grouping of unrelated or merely partly related businesses. We are one business and, for the most part, a business with a single mission.

Our job, and that of each division of IBM, is to help customers solve their problems through the use of data processing systems and other information-handling equipment. There is a close relationship between all the parts of our product line. Any major technological move or marketing decision in any one division is bound to have a direct effect on other segments of the business.

This means that decisions are being made constantly, all the way down the line, on matters that involve two or more divisions. One might suppose that burdensome machinery would have to be set up throughout the business to settle the thousands of small differences that could be expected to arise among the divisions.

To date it has not been necessary. No matter what division they may be in, basically all our managers are company-oriented. They think primarily in terms of what is good for IBM rather than what may be good for particular divisions. This may be so because many of them were with IBM long before we became a divisional organization. Many of our higher executives have incentive plans in addition to their salaries. But the plans are based on overall IBM performance rather than that of any single division. The arrangement, we believe, has helped to keep everyone pulling together.

Much of this we owe to the company's beliefs. Our people so thoroughly understand the need to give superior service that their concern for the well-being of the customer often overrides whatever differences of opinion there might be among them. Of course I do not mean that we have no differences. It is my responsibility, as it is the president's and that of the Corporate Management Committee, to resolve the major ones. By and large it hasn't been too bad.

As I said earlier, at the time of reorganization we suddenly found that we had need for a great many more staff experts and specialists than were on our rolls. In nearly every case we "made" these experts simply by naming a man to the job. We had some failures, but on the whole our method worked pretty well. The reason, I think, is that these young and relatively inexperienced executives knew three things as well as their own names:

—They knew that any decisions they might make and any actions they might take had to be right for our people.

—They knew that the main aim of our business is service, to help the customer solve his problems no matter how many problems this may create for us.

—And they knew that we will not settle for anything less than a superior effort in everything we do.

In other words, they understood our basic beliefs, and this understanding enabled them to move into unfamiliar jobs and to overcome the shortcomings they may have had in technical skills. This emphasis on beliefs is not meant to downgrade the importance of technical skill. But from the time of our divisional reorganization we have found that an ingrained understanding of the beliefs of IBM, far more than technical skill, has made it possible for our people to make the company successful.

In looking back on the history of a company, one can't help but reflect on what the organization has learned from its years in business. In thinking specifically of the period since the war when IBM faced the twin challenges of great technological change and growth, I would say that we've come out with five key lessons. They may not be applicable to all companies. All I can do is attest to the great value these five lessons had for us.

1. There is simply no substitute for good human relations and for the high morale they bring. It takes good people to do the jobs necessary to reach your profit goals. But good people alone are not enough. No matter how good your people may be, if they don't really like the business, if they don't feel totally involved in it, or if they don't think

they're being treated fairly—it's awfully hard to get a business off the ground. Good human relations are easy to talk about. The real lesson, I think, is that you must work at them all the time and make sure your managers are working with you.

2. There are two things an organization must increase far out of proportion to its growth rate if that organization is to overcome the problems of change. The first of these is communication, upward and downward. The second is education and retraining.

3. Complacency is the most natural and insidious disease of large corporations. It can be overcome if management will set the right tone and pace and if its lines of communication are in working order.

4. Everyone—particularly in a company such as IBM—must place company interest above that of a division or department. In an interdependent organization, a community of effort is imperative. Cooperation must outrank self-interest, and an understanding of the company's particular approach to things is more important than technical ability.

5. And the final and most important lesson: Beliefs must always come before policies, practices, and goals. The latter must always be altered if they

are seen to violate fundamental beliefs. The only sacred cow in an organization should be its basic philosophy of doing business.

The British economist Walter Bagehot once wrote: "Strong beliefs win strong men and then make them stronger." To this I would add, "And as men become stronger, so do the organizations to which they belong."

Part II

THE BROADER PURPOSE

6

CHANGING EXPECTATIONS

It would be shortsighted, I believe, to talk about
what I have learned in the management of a large
organization without also referring to what I have
come to believe is the place and responsibility of
such organizations in national life. In common with
most businessmen, I have formed some views on
how business can best fulfill its larger role as a part
of the nation.

It is in this area of the national well-being that
the business community will be judged most critically in the years ahead. Business has demonstrated
how successfully it can innovate and produce. What

we must now do—it would seem to me—is to assign a higher order of priority to the national interest in our business decisions.

The constant necessity to recognize public or national interest in all our business operations is a relatively new requirement for the businessman. Historically, we've always been able to count on the relatively free exercise of self-interest in our society to bring out what's best for all in the end. The manager of a large organization does what he thinks is best for his company. His competitors do what they think is best for theirs. Labor looks after itself; farmers do the same; and even government agencies develop ends of their own.

Out of the interplay of these forces in our economy there has developed a rather amazing system of checks and balances. As a result, all those forces usually complement one another and make each other stronger.

The system has its imperfections. Today, for example, it is entirely possible to have a contractual agreement between a very large company or industry and a very large union which will benefit both the industry and the union and at the same time have a detrimental effect upon the country as a whole. But we must never forget that the system works— it works and it produces. It produces more than any other economic system in the world. It spreads that production across our society in such a way that almost everyone benefits from it. Belief in the basic soundness and worth of our economic system does not, however, imply that it may never need adjustment. Conditions change. Expectations change.

The fact is that we have continually adjusted and improved our system in the past and must continue to do so. There never has been any future in the status quo. In business, the status quo means inevitable failure, and I would think the same conclusion could be drawn with nations.

Furthermore, what people expect from their society has been changing over the years. In the agrarian society of only a few generations ago, the demands of our citizens were relatively modest. But our society has altered in many ways since that time. In the light of these changes, it is necessary that we reexamine the basic premises on which

79

this society was laid down to see if we are meeting society's needs as well as we should by today's standards. This means that we must continually review the opportunities for all individuals in America. To some degree, of course, these opportunities are modified, beneficially or detrimentally, by the era of bigness in America—by big business, big government, big labor. Bigness itself is a relatively new phenomenon in our society. Even if nothing else had changed, the vast concentrations of power in our society would demand that businessmen reconsider their responsibilities for the broader public welfare.

More and more there seems to be entering into relationships between government, industry, and labor a fourth force—the force of the public. Anyone particularly interested in some segment of the economy must increasingly recognize the force of public or national interest. Ultimately we are held accountable to it. We exist at its tolerance. We are bound by its laws. In planning for the future of our own particular interest, we must recognize the rights and requirements of the public and the millions of individuals who make it up.

Changing Expectations

The theme of my remarks here is this: The several major elements that make up our American society are going to have to learn how to work together voluntarily and in partnership. Each must adjust its own interests to that of the public or risk one of two unpleasant alternatives—legislation which will make cooperation compulsory or internal division which will make it difficult for the United States to hold its world position.

In other words, we're going to have to learn to think in two dimensions: on one plane as a businessman, labor leader, or government official, each with his own particular point of view—on the second as a citizen whose first duty is not to a special interest but to the well-being of the whole nation.

A businessman's point of view, naturally, is business-oriented, as a government official's is oriented toward government and a labor leader's toward labor. Each must perform for his constituents or be voted out of office. But each, I submit, can pay attention to public need as well and still be successful.

I would be one of the first to admit that it's a good deal easier to state this proposition than to put it into practice. One of our most important continuing problems is the question of how we can strike a balance between what is sound business practice in the management of our large organizations and what is good for the national interest. It is a dilemma which will confront us more and more often in the years ahead.

How can the manager of a large organization run his business in the interests of his company and stockholders without, on occasion, doing something which is contrary to the broader interest of the United States? And whatever course the manager of a large organization elects to take, how can he be sure he is acting in such a way as to preserve his own freedom of decision in business matters?

Obviously this concept of self-restraint in the national interest introduces new problems into the already complicated business of corporate decision making. These are difficult questions—as difficult as any management has had to face, and they are made all the more difficult by the times in which we live.

Too often, I fear, we businessmen turn to conventional solutions when the world around us is demanding the very utmost in creativity, imagination, and boldness. Communists can't be dealt with on a business-as-usual basis. Our free society can survive, but not necessarily with the old ground rules. I believe we need new attitudes and new acts to meet new conditions.

The changed circumstances that make great co-operative effort necessary are not limited to the increasing threat from Communism—critical as that is.

Along with the growth of Soviet power, we are having to adjust ourselves to the economic recovery of Japan and Western Europe and the formation of new marketing alliances, particularly within the area of the Common Market. We face what some have called the "revolution of rising expectations" among the underdeveloped lands. We can no longer set the pace and timing of our national growth to suit ourselves.

These outside pressures make it necessary that we grow fast enough and in such a way as to command the respect of our enemies, the confidence of our friends, and the hopes of the underdeveloped nations.

83

We're competing in world power; we're competing in world trade; we're being asked to help bridge the gap between the rich nations and the poor nations by sharing our resources. All these activities have become vital to our national interest.

At home we must provide for the continuing cost of defense without neglecting our domestic social needs. How do we create a million and a half new jobs every year? How do we provide for the education we must have and for adequate medical care for all? These questions, too, are directly related to the national interest.

In addition, these domestic tasks are complicated by the population growth that has taken place in the United States. Some people contend that such things as unemployment insurance and old-age security are private concerns and should be left solely to private solutions. But just how realistic are these views in a nation which already has 187 million people and which will have 260 million by 1980? In a nation as large as this, hard times may befall only 5 per cent of the people. But today that 5 per cent represents 9 million people. And, very clearly, no nation can turn its back on the plight of 9 million people—their well-being is essential to the well-being of the nation.

Take all these tasks—the ones resulting from pressures outside, the ones resulting from pressures within—and you can see how new and huge are the problems that confront our society. To my way of thinking, we're going to have to look for improved ways of doing the job. And as a starter, I believe we're going to have to ask ourselves a little more seriously if what we are planning to do in our business decisions is as good for the employees as it is for the stockholders—and as good for the country as it is for both those groups.

Earlier, I tried to make the point that a business organization has need of a set of principles or beliefs to give it a common and consistent sense of direction. As conditions change, an organization must learn to accommodate change within the context of its beliefs. The same principle, I believe, holds true for our society as a whole.

Our national beliefs have come to us in many ways—some from documents like the Declaration of Independence, others from tradition, legislation, and practice. They survive because our people continue to value them. From them, I believe, comes much of the strength which moves the United States forward.

These beliefs are well known . . .

We believe in political and religious freedom and in the need to exercise these freedoms with responsibility.

We believe in a government of law to serve man and in the changeability of law to meet changed conditions.

We believe that society exists to help the individual better himself—intellectually, spiritually, and materially.

We believe in equality of opportunity and in extending a hand to help people to help themselves.

And finally, we believe in freedom of enterprise. We equate it with equal opportunity. We believe that everyone should have the opportunity to do as much as he can for himself with a minimum of interference and restriction.

There are some who might say that this last belief has fallen by the wayside, that businessmen are the only ones who really believe in it any longer. I don't think this is so. But I would agree that since most

Americans now work for someone else, they tend to look upon it a little differently than they might have a hundred years ago.

In the 1860s there was much government land to homestead. There were many avenues open to entrepreneurs at all economic and social levels, and millions took them. How very different is the United States today where eight out of ten people work for someone else—where thousands of factory workers can suddenly be laid off as a result of circumstances over which none has very much control.

Because they feel so vulnerable in the highly organized economic activity of today, most Americans insist that free enterprise so operate as to guarantee their right to such things as a job, a fair wage, humane working conditions, and old-age security. And when they feel that free enterprise comes into conflict with these wants, they line up solidly in defense of them. But this does not mean they have lost their belief in free enterprise. It simply means that they believe free enterprise must operate in a way that is reasonably compatible with these requirements.

Much as we may dislike it, I think we've got to

realize that in our kind of society there are times when government has to step in and help people with some of their more difficult problems. This does not mean that we have abandoned our traditional faith in American self-reliance. It means we have recognized that changing times have presented us with changing conditions which sometimes exceed the limits of self-reliance. And these changes are characteristic of a system as dynamic as ours.

Self-reliance cannot always provide an answer to every need, especially in a society as big as ours where people can get caught up in forces over which they have little personal control. Thrift is a necessary virtue, but there are times when even thrift does not make it possible for the ordinary family to cope with extraordinary problems.

Programs which assist Americans by reducing the hazards of a free market system without damaging the system itself are necessary, I believe, to its survival. If large numbers of people are made to feel that they're entirely at the mercy of that system or that they will be abandoned every time it undergoes one of its periodic adjustments, they can be expected to have less enthusiasm for the system than it deserves.

In acknowledging the need for some government intervention, it nevertheless is difficult for anyone to say what the proper limits of government in meeting these human needs should be. At what point does government weigh so heavily on the business system that it slows down our whole rate of economic growth? And at what point do social welfare programs begin to affect individual initiative and cause people to lose their incentive?

Obviously, there are no clear-cut answers. In a free society questions like these are resolved in the tug and pull of leadership and public opinion.

Businessmen, of course, are influential leaders in public opinion. That is why it is so important that they be as open-minded and far-sighted in matters concerning the general public need as they are in questions relating to the operation of their businesses.

To be sure, the rights and guarantees that the average man believes in and insists upon may interfere, to some degree, with our ability to manage our enterprises with complete freedom of action. As a result, there are businessmen who either ignore or deny these claims. They then justify their views by contending that if we were to recognize or grant them, the whole system of free enterprise would be endangered.

This, it would seem to me, amounts to an open invitation to exactly the kind of government intervention that businessmen are seeking to avoid. For if we businessmen insist that free enterprise permits us to be indifferent to those things on which people put high value, then the people will quite naturally assume that free enterprise has too much freedom. And since the people have voting power, they will move against free enterprise to curtail it in their own interests. They do this, however, not because they are opposed to free enterprise, but to obtain and, in some cases, to protect the rights they believe themselves entitled to under a free enterprise system.

Historically, I think we can show that restraints on business have not come into being simply because someone wanted to make life harder for us businessmen. In almost every instance they came about because businessmen had put such emphasis on self-interest that their actions were regarded as objectionable and intolerable by the people and their elected representatives.

For centuries the businessman has been a favorite whipping boy, and the reasons are plain to see. Businessmen acquired wealth. With wealth, they gained power. And until this century, much of that power was employed almost solely in their own interests.

Despite its historical abuses of power, business has always been one of the world's great forward forces. The business record in the United States is one in which we can all take pride. As much as any other group, we have helped to build this country's national power. And as much as any group, we have helped to provide the great opportunities which exist in the American society. Furthermore, I believe that American industry—as much as any other single force—has within it the solutions to our present peril.

In spite of these many achievements we still have a mixed business legacy, whether we like it or not. We are all familiar with the freewheeling actions of big business in the half century following the Civil War.

Interestingly, as these excesses got out of hand, a public reaction set in. In 1888 all the political parties closed ranks to demand Federal restraints on business. Two years later we had the Sherman Antitrust Act. And although it was little used in those early days, it did establish one telling proposition: Business is subject not only to existing law—but to the tolerance of the public. Lawful or not, if business does things which the public regards as wrong and abusive, that public has the power to demand new laws with which business will have to comply.

This proposition was reaffirmed again and again during and after the early 1900s. In law after law Congress upheld the principle that business operates at the tolerance of the public, and that freedom of enterprise does not grant business the license to trespass on what the government regards as the public interest.

My own company became involved with the Antitrust Division in 1952, and we now operate under a consent decree. It never seemed to me that this action gave me grounds to criticize the government. In fact I have frequently stated that I believed the law was a force for good and that I have no quarrel with the decision in relation to IBM.

With the onset of the Great Depression in the 1930s a new consideration came into the picture. People were not only angered by what they regarded as the excesses of business—they were critical of a system which failed to provide old-age security, unemployment compensation, and such things as fair standards in wages and hours. In the changed context of the times they now saw all these as their rights. They therefore insisted on them, in the light of their new beliefs, and they demanded and got a whole new pattern of social legislation.

This, too, should have taught us a lesson. It should have reminded us that when people insist on social betterment and justice they are not going to be dissuaded by cries of alarm at what they may be doing to the free enterprise system. They look on the system as a changing institution—one which must change with the times. And as their needs become greater, or as their wants and ambitions grow, they demand new laws and programs—trusting in the ability of that free enterprise system to bear the costs.

What we must always remember is that countries and systems exist for the benefit of their people. If a system does not measure up to the growing expectations of those people, they will move to modify or change it. To keep faith in our business system and to help build our country, the best thing we can do is to make our system work so that everyone shares fairly in it. We won't build good citizenship and we won't build a strong country by holding people back. We will build by helping people to enlarge their goals and to achieve them.

7

NEW PROBLEMS, NEW APPROACHES

We all know that special power imposes special responsibilities on those who hold it. In asking ourselves how we can make business decisions with a proper regard for the public interest, let us examine the attitude and performance of some American business executives.

No one denies that the managers of our large organizations have acquired powers which extend far beyond their offices and plants. They exercise great influence in their communities, their states, the nation. Nor is there any reason why they should not, for they have shown—in the words of Du Pont's Crawford Greenewalt—that they are "Uncommon Men."

Yet there is the businessman who, when he hears of a legislative proposal having to do with some domestic program of social welfare, too often stiffens his back and takes a position which is so predictable as to be almost automatic:

If the program costs money, he is against it.

If it means more government, he is against it.

And if the wrong party has proposed it, he is certain it's no good.

This is hardly the way for a leadership group to act if it wishes to command respect. Certainly we are never going to live up to our special responsibilities if we are doctrinaire rather than objective every time issues of this kind come up. If the American people ever come to believe that we businessmen can always be counted on to shout "No!" they will not only regard us as being against them—they will cease to have respect for our opinions. And should the time come when our opinions mean nothing, we businessmen will have forfeited our claim to leadership in the United States.

It's time we realized that a stubborn doctrinaire approach to these matters is not only bad for the country; it's equally bad for business. If we ever seem to oppose all forms of social welfare, then the American people can hardly be blamed if they seem insensitive to our pleas for the protection of our business system.

Certainly we don't behave in this same narrow-minded way in the running of our businesses. We examine our problems. We ask ourselves what has to be done. We work up several alternatives. We recheck the costs. And then we make decisions on what to do.

Why wouldn't the same kind of an approach to national problems or legislation be a constructive one for business and the nation? We could begin by examining the situation to see whether there actually is a problem and how serious it may be. Then we could ask ourselves if the solution which has been proposed is a good one. If we have doubts, let's not reject the whole program out of hand. Let's look for alternatives. Let's show the public that we are aware of the problems and that we are *for* some means of coming to grips with them.

If we are reasonable in our approach, and if we conclude that a specific proposal is bad for the country as well as for business, we can oppose the proposition on far firmer ground.

Unfortunately, the American people have little reason to feel reassured by what they've been hearing from businessmen on social legislation during the last twenty or thirty years. More often than not the bills have been bitterly attacked—and the attacks have been anything but constructive.

In the mid-thirties, for example, when social security legislation was proposed, the business reaction was largely negative. A spokesman for one business organization went so far as to predict that social security would mean the "ultimate socialistic control of life and industry" in the United States.

And in the same period, when a law was proposed to regulate the activities of the stock exchange after the debacle of 1929, one business leader said flatly that the bill was designed to push the nation "along the road from Democracy to Communism."

Despite the great progress which has been made since the enactment of those laws and many others, we still hear echoes of the thirties in the voices of some businessmen. Only recently, when the Social Security Act was broadened to include more people and provide for increased benefits, too much of the reaction from business sounded as if it came from the past.

When we act this way, we show a peculiar ambivalence which must be puzzling to our friends. As businessmen, we are innovators and we take great pride in such things as technological improvements. Yet when it comes to social problems, we seem curiously unwilling on too many occasions to risk any kind of innovation. More often than not, the consensus overrides us anyhow and those bills we opposed become law. Then we find ourselves helping to make the whole thing practicable by building an economy which can support those programs. In a sense, we appear to be holding the clock back, when actually we are the force that makes it possible for the clock to move forward.

What makes this posture all the more ironic is that the American businessman, almost always a conservative in national affairs, is the world's champion problem-solver in his own shop. I propose again that we carry the same attitude to national affairs, where problem-solving is ever more vital.

In matters relating to the liberalization of social security, for example, I suspect that ten years hence business will thoroughly approve the measures many businessmen opposed in 1961 or 1962, just as we now are glad to have most of the social security legislation we opposed so bitterly in the 1930s.

On a question like Federal aid to education, we've got to ask ourselves whether existing patterns of local taxation and state aid can meet the increasing costs of better schooling. There is a great disparity in what states now spend on education. Some spend more than twice as much per pupil as do others. Is it right that some children should be penalized simply because they happen to live in a locality which may lack the tax base for adequate school financing?

I don't think we can dismiss the problem simply by saying let the localities face up to it themselves. Of course, local solutions are desirable, and I would be one of the first to vote for them and against Federal aid, if they can be made to work. Yet some localities are apparently unequal to the task. We are going to have to find a better way to help those communities do the job.

The quality of education has become a critical factor in national strength. This consideration, to my way of thinking, far outweighs any fears I might have about Federal aid to education. The important thing in a situation like this is to solve the problem and to solve it by the *best* means, even if this does call for some change in tradition.

On the question of national health problems, again we've got to think in terms of solutions rather than in terms of the dangers some may see in present propositions. We can't simply say that inadequate medical care is the price people must pay if they are incapable of earning enough to provide for themselves.

Closer to home for the businessman are the complex and interconnected problems of unemployment, automation, and expanding population. Here the businessman plays a direct part in the problem as well as its solution.

One of the great contradictions in our affluent society is unemployment. One can quarrel with the statistics, but all that does is to change the total.

What's left is still intolerable for a country like ours. We can't hide the problem by doubting the statistics any more than we can say it doesn't exist because our wives cannot hire maids. It is with us and it has been with us for too many years. We've got to find some better solution to it, through business as well as government action.

In fairness to the businessman, it should be stated that during the last twenty years he has been remarkably attentive to the needs of his employees. Broad benefit programs are now the norm for most big business organizations. Great efforts are being made to spread the work and eliminate unnecessary lay-offs. Many businessmen have accepted the fact that out-of-the-ordinary medical costs, adequate insurance, and adequate provision for retirement are beyond the means of the average employee. To close these gaps, we have introduced benefit programs and are making improvements in them all the time.

If we grant that these programs are necessary and right for the employees of big corporations, then certainly we cannot follow a double standard and contend that they are not needed by other people. Only 14 per cent of the total United States work force is employed by the top 500 industrial corporations. Some provisions should be made to give all some fair measure of protection.

The manager of a large organization may have done a fine job in demonstrating what he can do for his people. But let him go one step beyond this and recognize that people who are not working for large organizations—or those who are not working at all—may have even greater need for partial assistance with some of their problems than his employees do. He might well remember this before he automatically criticizes a piece of legislation aimed at helping those people.

Most of these comments have had to do with how I think businessmen are going to have to change their way of looking at things if this country —and its business system—are to get through the difficulties we foresee in the years ahead.

Some people, I'm afraid, may have the impression that I'm so preoccupied with these larger problems of the national and public interest that I've forgotten what the first function of the businessman is —to run his business and make a success of it.

Of course I haven't—not for a single moment. If the businessman fails at business, then all his other concerns will mean nothing, for he will have lost the power to do anything about them.

But, by the same token, I do believe we can make just as big a mistake by concentrating on the running of our businesses to the exclusion of these broader considerations of the public good. I think we can render to our stockholders that which is theirs and at the same time do what we think is best for the country without bringing the two into head-on conflict.

This does not mean that we're all going to find a middle ground where we shall live with one another happily ever after. Even in a middle ground there is a wide range of choice between what we regard as the preservation of self-interest and a genuine concern for the national well-being.

There is a place for the liberals who will press for faster progress just as there is a place for the conservatives who will hold for caution. But even as we rule out the extremists on the left who would torpedo the whole business system, so must we also rule out those on the right who would turn the calendar back to a make-believe age which never really existed.

Individuals and organizations have failed because they have been ahead of their times. But many more have failed because they have been *behind* their times, because they have been unwilling to pull their heads out of the sand and accept the reality of change.

I have said that there have been many instances in which businessmen have fought the wrong kind of a stubborn rear-guard action against the inevitability of social change. But in wartime, when the issue becomes one of life or death for the nation, businessmen have always moved to a position of open-minded leadership. They have shown boldness and creativity which contributed in a major way to all our victories.

The guns aren't firing now; nevertheless, we are in a mortal contest. We are in a war of ideas and a war of national performance which in many ways is more serious than any open conflict we have known. It poses great new challenges and opportunities for American businessmen.

Rich as our economy is, it will never be rich

enough to afford unnecessary division in times like these. There have already been too many down-turns, too little growth. If we are to meet our responsibilities and hold our place in the world, we're going to have to make this society of ours function more effectively than it does now by reconciling our differences and achieving greater accord with one another in the national interest.

Businessmen aren't the only ones at fault, and they can't effect this change alone; every other element of our society is going to have to do its part. But someone is going to have to start, someone is going to have to set a standard—and this, I believe, we businessmen can do.

We have to learn how to live with and how to respond in the national interest to the protracted struggle in which we are engaged with the Soviets.

We have to learn how to live with and how to respond in the national interest to the competitive challenge that has come about with modernization in the industrial plants of Western Europe and Japan.

We have to learn how to live with and how to respond in the national interest to the profound changes that are taking place in our own society as we grow toward a highly interdependent population of 260 million by 1980.

We've come a long way since the reformation of the 1930s, the end of isolationism in the 1940s, the beginning of a new technological age in the 1950s. We've resolved many problems, but we've created many new ones—many of them more critical and on a far larger scale.

As America meets the challenges of today and tomorrow, as she succeeds in critical and difficult areas, she will do so more and more because of business leadership and not in spite of it. This is the promise of the future.

ABOUT THE AUTHOR

The personalities of corporations and their founders are often inseparable; one is frequently an extension of the other. Certainly this was true of IBM and Thomas J. Watson, Sr. They combined to make an American business legend. This legend continued into a second generation under the firm hand of Thomas J. Watson, Jr.

A better than two-billion dollar a year global business, the present IBM is as different from the IBM of a relatively few years ago as the prewar America is from today. It was the younger Watson who played a large hand in fitting the company to the changed environment.

He was born in Dayton, Ohio in 1914 and made his first speech at an IBM sales meeting when he was twelve. After graduating from Brown University in 1937, Watson became an IBM salesman in downtown Manhattan. Fourteen months before the United States entered World War II, he went on active service and became a B-24 pilot. An airplane enthusiast, he had been flying since his college years.

During the period before the war, Thomas J. Watson, Jr. had more than held his own in a company that prides itself on salesmanship. In 1946 he was made a vice president. He became president in 1952, chief executive officer in 1956, and continued in that latter post as chairman of the board until 1971, a year after suffering a heart attack.

Like his father, Watson's interests ranged beyond his corporation to wide areas of public concern. He served as a trustee of a number of organizations and was a member of the President's Advisory Committee on Labor-Management Policy.

Watson died in Greenwich, Connecticut, on December 31, 1993 of complications following a stroke. He was seventy-nine.

CPSIA information can be obtained at www.ICGtesting.com
Printed in the USA
LVOW072133171011

250936LV00001B/41/P